8 Lies Used By Gun-Grabbers

In light of the gun-grabbing fascists ramping up their efforts to strip Americans of their natural rights to property and self-defense, I've compiled a list of what seem to be the eight most common, immoral, deceptive lies told by authoritarians who seek to take guns from individuals and leave them only in the hands of the government/police. As I was about to publish this on LibertyBlock.com, I learned that retired supreme court justice John Paul Stevens, a hero to the radical Democrats wrote an op-ed today calling for the repealing of the second amendment.

Yes, the timing is ironic. No, I'm not sure whether I'm surprised, (he practically asserted this years ago in his Heller dissent) and I will not really address that authoritarian bastard in this article. If you want to know my opinion of him, you need only to look back to the 4th and 5th to last words in the prior sentence.

Onto the list:

1) Gun-grabbers say: "Crossing an international border shouldn't make someone into a criminal!"

But crossing a **state** border while legally carrying a pistol should make someone into a criminal! Those who cross from a pro-gun state into a leftist state (like NY, NJ, CA, CT, MA, etc.) may serve decades in prison for doing nothing other than carrying a pistol like they do every day in their home state)

Ironic bonus hypocrisy: A man who was deported 5 times for previous crimes crossed from Mexico into California illegally, obtained a pistol illegally, and then killed[1] an innocent young woman. California acquitted him of murder and manslaughter. The defense hardly even disputed the actions he was charged with. He was guilty. And he had been deported for crimes 5 times in the past. Even Judge Andrew Napolitano, an open-borders advocate, called for the killer to be prosecuted and referred to him as a "serious and imminent threat[2]".

2) Gun-grabbers say: "Not all illegal immigrants are criminals!"

But Leftists do believe that ALL Americans who exercise their natural rights ARE criminals, and should be treated as such. After one psychotic/evil murderer reportedly killed 17 students in a Florida high school last month, the Democrat elites began spending millions of dollars convincing concerned yet naive Americans to protest in order to call for the government to take natural and constitutional rights away from innocent people like you and me.

Ironic Bonus hypocrisy: Democrats opposed[3] illegal immigration just a few years ago. Today, the Democrat platform supports zero border control existing on the southern border of the US, and zero restrictions on people entering the US, and few restrictions on them obtaining welfare.

3) Gun-grabbers say: "Gun free zones decrease gun crime!"

Actually, statistics[4] show that over 98% of mass shootings occur in gun free zones.

4) Gun-grabbers say: "Strict gun laws (like Chicago has) make cities much safer!"

Actually, Chicago has infinitely more shootings[5] and shooting deaths than any other city in the US.

5) Gun-grabbers say: "The more guns individuals own, the more violent crime occurs!"

It takes only a few minutes of research to learn that the more gun freedom/more guns exist in a state, the lower the gun crime. New Hampshire and Wyoming have essentially no restrictions on guns, each state has many more guns than citizens, and they consistently enjoy the lowest murder rates in the US. Remember, Chicago has essentially zero 'legal' guns, and has already had over 500 shootings in 2018.

6) Gun-grabbers say: "Only police should have guns! People can't be trusted to use them judiciously!"

There are far too many cases of cops using their guns to murder people in cold blood. And there are many more that don't make the news. And they are almost never punished for using their guns to hurt or kill innocent people.

I have had a difficult time determining whether NYC[6], Maricopa County[7], or Miami[8] has the most unjust police force. Some police departments literally act like violent gangs; they use their guns to break into stores[9], terrorize people, smash the surveillance cameras, and steal the products. The NYPD uses its monopoly on authority and gun ownership to conduct a massive gun-running scheme[10], in which they exchange gun permits for bribes. Maybe that's why the NYPD supports such strict gun control. The Baltimore Police carry realistic-looking lookalike guns[11] on them in order to plant them on suspects. The Salt Lake City Police use their guns to force people to violate[12] the 4th and 5th amendment rights of trauma patients.

These are just a few examples of many that would make it seem quite difficult to consider American police departments to be 'judicious'.

Civilians actually spend an incredible amount of time and money on training, holsters, and other equipment to guarantee that they are always practicing extremely safe firearms etiquette. If gun owners in the US were more focused on using them for violence than using them safely, this video[13] wouldn't have over 11 million views. If the Democratic propaganda about gun owners were true, we wouldn't watch and upload millions of videos on how to carry safely.

7) Gun-grabbers say: "Only police can utilize firearms safely!" They are too dangerous for civilians!

There are far too many cases of police officers misusing their firearms so pathetically that even a toddler would reprimand them. And many such cases surely don't make the news. This cop[14] and this cop[15] have fired their guns unintentionally in classrooms full of kids. Some cops load AR-15s, deploy them, and then leave[16] them lying in the street in front of the public.

8) "Stop being a cowboy. Just call the police if you're ever in danger. Police will come and protect you!"

Oyyyy. This is another great one. For starters, the average police response time to even the highest priority calls is much greater than 2 minutes (7 minutes?). Mathematically, if police cannot travel faster than 1200 feet per second and they are not closer to you than the attacker is, they cannot help you until after you've been shot. Protect yourself. Don't rely on them. Speaking of which, cops don't actually have any duty to protect you. Nope. The Supreme Court of the United States[17] has ruled that they do not. Their only duty is to arrest people for crimes, not to protect people/stop crimes. If you want protection, look into the Glock 19 for yourself.

Bonus hypocrisy: The left has been loudly yelling since Trump's election that he is reminiscent of Hitler and that his administration is evil, oppressive, and tyrannical. Why, then, does the left support the federal government (and state and local governments) having all of the firepower and the individuals having none? Why is the left and their hero favorite Supreme Court Justice calling for the repeal of the 2nd amendment[18] entirely?

5 Good Things Trump Did

After a year and a half in office, I think that I've seen enough to make a judgement on President Trump: He is wildly unpredictable and may have zero consistent principles.

Other than perhaps 'America First', Trump seems to flip back and forth on every major (and minor) issue. Trump campaigned on non-interventionism and then continued to bomb nearly every country that Obama did. He campaigned massively on ending all illegal immigration and totally ending DACA, and then offered amnesty to millions of 'Dreamers' and continues nearly the exact same immigration policies that Obama had in place (which involved millions of deportations[19], unbeknownst to many Americans). He has flipped from supporting absolute gun rights to supporting stricter gun control than anything passed even by Obama - and boasting about it. He has flipped on marijuana[20] policy, taxes, and so many other issues. Many people say that Trump often agrees with and implements the proposals of the last person he speaks with. This may be true. He may actually hold zero consistent principles. As the old joke (attributed to Groucho Marx) goes: "These are my principles. If you don't like them, I have others." All in all, Trump has made some very good and very bad decisions in his first 18 months in office. As such, we've written this article which focuses on the good and another one which focuses on the bad.

The Good

1) SCOTUS
Following the peculiar and sudden death of conservative Supreme Court Justice Antonin Scalia, the nation worried about which type of judge the unpredictable, unprincipled president would nominate to fill the vacancy. In a very pleasant surprise to conservatives (and many libertarians), President Trump nominated Neil Gorsuch, who was confirmed by the Senate to fill the seat previously held by Scalia. Gorsuch has since ruled in favor of removing the federal ban[21] on sports betting and ruled that a car being a rental does not give police the power to search the car without a warrant[22]. It seems early, but Gorsuch may be one of the better pro-freedom justices we have. Trump has also appointed many great judges to the lower federal courts, from what I've heard. In a world where judges create laws by setting precedents, Trump appointing solid constitutional jurists to federal courts could do a lot to reverse the nation's spiral into authoritarian socialism.

2) Tax Reform?
I know many people who would consider putting this one in the 'bad' column. In fact, I am one of those people! While the TCJA did maintain the 70,000+ page tax code and upheld the use of tax code to manipulate[23] human behavior, simply put - it cut taxes for most Americans. Of the 7 federal income tax brackets, 5 of them were decreased. The tax on businesses was also decreased from 35% to 21%. This will result in increased wages and has already resulted in billions of dollars in bonuses[24] for American workers. By allowing entrepreneurs to keep more of their earned money, the new tax code should give a significant stimulus to businesses which could be used to reinvest, expand, decrease prices of products, hire workers, and increase wages. This was the first time that federal taxes were decreased at all in decades. Technically speaking, however, the tax cuts for businesses were permanent and the tax cuts for individuals were temporary (sunset).

3) De-regulation
In a world where every local and national government seems to be increasing regulations on every aspect of daily life, Trump keeping his promise to decrease regulations was an amazingly liberating breath of fresh air. Under Obama, the EPA created 4,400 new laws. The US currently has millions - or perhaps billions of laws and regulations. That's the thing; there are now too many[25] laws and regulations to even count. In 2012, regulations cost small manufacturers over $2 trillion, according to this NAM study[26]. Only days after assuming the presidency, Trump signed an executive order directing federal agencies to cut two regulations[27] for every one new regulation added. While I was quite skeptical of how substantial this would turn out to be, I was extremely excited to see a government official - especially the president - actively decreasing government power. Apparently, agencies outperformed the 2:1 ratio by a massive margin[28]. This is one of the most pro-America and pro-freedom events to occur in my lifetime. Thanks to President Trump, if you begin a business tomorrow, you will have much less red tape holding you back from engaging in free market commerce with other consenting adults.

4) Appointed/Nominated Pro-Freedom Officials
While Trump did nominate some horrible, authoritarian, corrupt individuals, he did seem to make some pretty libertarian picks right off the bat, as well. Some of his first nominations included Betsy Devos, a woman who is hated by the Democrats for supporting alternatives to strict federal education curricula to be secretary of education. Devos and Trump have culled the federal education budget (which should be $0 according to the Constitution and according to common libertarian sense) and relinquished some federal powers back to states so that each state can guide its education policy. Trump appointed Scott Pruitt to head the EPA. The fact that Pruitt had sued the EPA and apparently said that the agency "should not exist" made me extremely happy. The EPA should not exist. Especially not on a federal level. And especially not without a constitutional amendment creating the new agency. While Rick Perry, the former governor of Texas may not be the most principled pro-freedom politician, I was excited to hear that Trump nominated a person who had once said that the federal Energy Department should not exist to run the department. I agree that the federal government has no business interfering with my energy.

I don't know much about Mick Mulvaney, but I remember my first thoughts when I heard that Trump appointed the congressman to the position of 'White House Budget Director' (and then to director of the CFPB, as well). I recognized the name from a short while prior, when the EpiPen scandal[29] broke onto the forefront of the news. Much like the recent congressional granstan- I mean, hearings where congressmen yelled at Mark Zuckerberg for collecting and misusing tons of personal data of Americans (which was obviously incredibly ironic), congressmen grilled the Mylan CEO, Heather Bresch for being so uncompassionate in her increasing of the prices of the EpiPen. The only person that I heard employ any logic during the scandal was congressman Mick Mulvaney. Instead of insinuating that the federal government controls the epinephrine industry, he pondered whether corruption was involved in the massive price-gouging scheme. Of course, corruption was very likely involved.

And we already mentioned Gorsuch and the other pro-freedom judges that Trump has seemingly appointed.

5) Gave land back to Utah (which Obama had stolen)
This is an issue that few people have heard of. Although I am not the most informed political analyst in the world, I do remember being infuriated that Obama stole land from Utah just before leaving office. I also remember being ecstatic when I heard that Trump gave it back. In the final weeks of his presidency, Obama reappropriated[30] over 1.35 million acres away from Utah and 300,000 acres away from Nevada to the federal government. Simply put, this was an annexation of land. Of course, Obama and the Democrats claimed that Utah and Nevada were too stupid to care for their public land; that only the federal government was responsible[31] enough to protect it. Ten months after assuming office, Trump decreased the size[32] of the new federal 'Bear's Ears' monument in Utah by 85% and returned other federal land to the state of Utah. This was when I realized that regardless of the many horrible, corrupt, authoritarian policies that Trump was maintaining, he is the first president in a very long time that has the capacity to decrease the power of the federal government.

Note: I purposely neglected to address foreign policy, since I believe that those who do not work in the State Dept., White House, CIA, or Pentagon probably know little to nothing about what is actually occurring in regards to foreign policy. Obama's foreign policy seemed horrible, and Trump is probably not changing foreign policy much. That's all I'll say about that.
I also did not touch on immigration, because I apparently have an incredibly unique perspective on immigration policy, and my honest opinions on it would probably make 99% of The Liberty Block's readers (most of which are libertarian) turn on me. And I simply don't have the inclination to take on that discussion at the moment.

I hope that you found this article insightful and please comment below with your thoughts!
Thank you very much!

<u>5 Bad Things Trump Did</u>

After a year and a half in office, I think that I've seen enough to make a judgement on President Trump: He is wildly unpredictable and may have zero consistent principles.

1) Increased Civil Asset Forfeiture

In July of 2017, The Washington Post[33] reported that Trump and his Attorney General were enacting a new plan to increase the legalized theft perpetrated by law enforcement, known as 'civil asset forfeiture'. The practice involves local, state, or federal law enforcement stealing money, guns, drugs, or any other form of property from individuals based only on suspicion that the property might somehow be involved in a crime. This is not the same as taking the heroin from dealers once they are convicted and sent to prison. This is not simply taking guns from violent gang leaders after they are charged with mass murder. This theft occurs without any convictions, warrants, or even charges being filed against a person. Indeed, law enforcement officers can take any property they wish, as long as they state that they believe that the property could somehow theoretically be involved in some crime in the past, present, or future. Trump, Sessions, and the DOJ are now encouraging state and local law enforcement to steal even more than in the past using this criminal practice. We'll circle back to government officials taking things from citizens without due process later on in the article.

2) Appointed/Nominated Authoritarians & Cronies

In addition to nominating Jeff Sessions (who had previously been a politician for 43 years) to be the Attorney General (the head of the DOJ), President Trump appointed many other authoritarians and political cronies to high positions - just like every president in modern times surely has. Trump nominated his friend and Exxon CEO, Rex Tillerson to be Secretary of State. I didn't trust Tillerson. A little over a year later, Trump asked Tillerson to resign and replaced him with CIA Director, Mike Pompeo. I don't trust him either. Trump made Gina Haspel the new CIA director. I don't trust her, either. Trump appointed Elaine Chao, the wife of the most powerful man in the US Senate to be secretary of transportation. I don't trust her, either. If you are beginning to notice that I don't generally trust powerful Washington politicians, you'd be correct. Trump has appointed many officials[34] in his first 18 months, most of whom I know much too little about to judge. I assume that most are typical politicians and that at least some are purely evil authoritarians. Some, however, seem to support freedom in some instances. We'll get to those officials later in the article.

3) Omnibus/Spending

Despite claiming to be 'unhappy' about it, Trump signed a $1.3 trillion omnibus spending bill, which funded the federal government for the year. In addition to being horribly reckless and authoritarian, omnibus bills are illegal. Yet, they have been common practice in Washington for decades. Trump ran his campaign on fiscal responsibility, yet he signed the largest spending bill in US history. Despite campaigning as the ultimate pro-life and low-tax candidate, Trump's first spending bill continued to give federal taxpayer dollars to Planned Parenthood, the nation's largest abortion provider. This 2,232-page spending bill was written by leadership (great Americans like Schumer, McConnell, and Pelosi wrote this bill) and was only given to the legislators hours before the vote was to take place - meaning that they could not possibly read it before they voted on it. In this interview, US Senator Mike Lee explains that the US government is no longer representative of the American people. A few thousand voters elect representatives who then 'represent' hundreds of thousands of people. Even those representatives do not actually have a say in writing the important bills and they sometimes can't even read the bills until hours before the vote takes place. Congressman Massie and other congressmen explain in this new series just how little power our representatives have in passing laws. From what I understand, spending under Trump continues to increase rapidly every year, just like it has for decades. Vetoing the omnibus bill would have been the perfect opportunity for Trump to show that he was different, demonstrate his libertarian doctrine on spending, and it would have been the ultimate 'screw you' to the establishment which has grown accustomed to writing these massive spending package bills and then forcing them into law.

4) Market Intervention

Conservatives generally claim to support a totally free market, meaning an economy with no government involvement. Trump's campaign seemed to have a more 'America first' feel to it than a 'free market' feel. Trump often mentioned in campaign speeches that he will use his governmental powers to ensure that businesses remain in the US. In this instance, Trump has generally kept his word. As promised, Trump did convince[35] the air conditioning goliath, Carrier, to remain in the US despite their plan to move manufacturing to the cheaper labor market in Mexico. Many conservatives willfully ignore how he accomplished this, though. This was accomplished by threatening massive tariffs on the company in the event that they moved some production out of the US. Tariffs result in increased costs for the end-consumer, which would be Americans, in this case. Trump has also been meddling in Amazon's business and he's imposed tariffs on foreign products that have hurt Americans instead of helping them. I believe that the less the government interferes with the market, the more prosperous (and free) the people will be.

5) Trump Violated The 2nd Amendment

On at least 2 occasions, President Trump has demonstrated his disregard for the 2nd amendment (as well as property rights and self-defense rights). In the wake of the tragic mass shootings in Nevada and Florida, some politicians began to support laws that empowered law enforcement officials to confiscate firearms from people who seemed dangerous. 'Red flag laws' circumvent the need for due process, in which a standard warrant, conviction, or proof of insanity might be required in order to confiscate someone's property. In February, Trump said that he wants law enforcement to take firearms[36] away from individuals before due process occurs, without any charges, warrants, or convictions against the person.

In March, Trump tweeted that he had directed the ATF to reclassify bump stocks so that they could be regulated/banned by the federal government. Could the ATF do this? Even the Obama-Holder administration, the most anti-gun administration I've ever known admitted that such a law could not be created by a federal agency. They believed that the House and Senate would be required in order to pass such a law. They are all incorrect, however. Even Congress cannot make any laws regarding weapons without first passing a constitutional amendment. A simple bill would not suffice. This wildly authoritarian decision by President Trump earned him his first 'Statist of the Month' award from The Liberty Block. If this results in federal 'red flag laws' passing or if the ATF does execute Trump's plan to redefine bump stocks, Trump will have passed more gun control than President Obama.

Note: I purposely neglected to address foreign policy, since I believe that those who do not work in the State Dept., White House, CIA, Pentagon, etc. probably know little to nothing about what is actually occurring in regards to foreign policy. Obama's foreign policy seemed horrible, and Trump is probably not changing much of it. That's all I know.

I also did not touch on immigration, because I seemingly have a unique and offensive perspective on immigration policy, and my honest opinions on the matter would be best explained in another article.

NH Police Waging War on Privacy

In June, The Liberty Block reported that the Lincoln Police became the first department in New Hampshire to utilize automatic license plate readers on their vehicles after the legislature repealed the state ban (largely due to pressure from NH police chiefs) on their use in 2016. Since then, at least one more - the Sunapee Police Department[37] has begun to utilize this Orwellian device in the name of public safety. We have heard reports that many other police departments in NH are planning to buy license plate readers for their vehicles over the next few years.

As reported by NHPR.org[38], license plate scanners in Vermont scanned 7.9 million license plates (over 12 times the entire population of Vermont) in the 18 months preceding 2013. This was accomplished using only 61 police-car-mounted LPRs in the entire state. According to the VPR study, the recordings have remained in a central law enforcement database along with the time and location. Simply put, this means that nearly everyone in Vermont is being tracked by law enforcement, and their whereabouts and daily routines are now known to their government and police.

Despite its supposed use - to keep communities safe - the new technology has not led to any increase in arrests or tickets for the crimes that it is capable of detecting since they were first utilized in 2009, according to VPR.

If they aren't even helping police, why would they expect us to sacrifice our privacy?

On the topic of LPR use by police in Vermont, Allen Gilbert, ACLU Director of Vermont said "A citizen's right to privacy is violated whenever a government records movements of individuals who are not subjects of an investigation." and "After a while, a whole series of bits of information about us can paint a pretty detailed picture of where we've been."

Under Vermont law, the recordings are only to be kept in the database for 18 months. Under the new NH program, recordings must be erased within 3 minutes. Do we have any reason to trust politicians and police though?

The politicians and police who wish to steal our privacy and convert it into power for themselves claim that LPRs are only a minimal infringement on our privacy and that they will only be used against dangerous criminals. Mark my words: Within a decade, every single time your car moves, the government and law enforcement will know exactly where you're going. In 1913, the US government created the federal income tax. They were successful in passing a new tax because the brackets were only 1% to 7%[39] at the time. Today, those brackets are 10% to 37%.

In 1950, only one in twenty workers in the US needed the government's permission (occupational license) to work. Now, nearly one in three people need the government's permission to work.

Government programs that take liberty from citizens only grow. They never shrink and they never even seem to remain stagnant.

Privacy and freedom in New Hampshire are dying. Actually, they're being taken by law enforcement and politicians. The Liberty Block plans to help reinstate the ban on automatic license plate scanners in the 2019 legislative session, but we need your help! Email and call your state representatives and senators as much as you need to until they agree to reinstate the ban on this horrific technology being utilized against innocent people by police. For the time being, we strongly recommend buying some sort of privacy screen for your license plate. Let's not make it easier than we need to for these corrupt tyrants to track our every move!

Toxic Masculinity - The Ultimate Divider

Authoritarian socialists may be evil, but they are not stupid. They understand very well how effective the oft-used tactic of 'divide and conquer' could be. Indeed, if Americans are fighting among themselves, they are less likely to fight the authoritarian politicians who control the nation. Left-wing authoritarians have used race to divide Americans. While it had some success, this tactic has two flaws: Americans from NYC to Wyoming are becoming more accepting and tolerant of people of all races and religions. (Yes, I have seen this with my own eyes) Secondly, race relations are largely irrelevant within homogeneous communities like the Bronx or those in northern Maine. The tactic simply does not affect enough people. Politicians have used social/financial status to divide Americans and turn them against one another. This also achieved a degree of success, especially among millenials. Hating Richie McWealthy is easy, but many, if not most people secretly (or openly) strive to become wealthy themselves. Many Americans do not engage in class warfare to the extent that the communist politicians long for. These tyrants are persistent and committed to discovering a divider that could affect every human being in the US. Finally, they've realized it: every human in the US is a male or a female (though, ironically, the radical left has begun to vehemently deny this). Could that scientific fact be utilized for their evil purpose?

Enter: Toxic masculinity
The leftist politicians and activists have seemingly settled on 'toxic masculinity' for their next attempt. Actually, it is hardly a new concept. In fact, it meshes quite well with the increasingly radical leftist concept that is increasingly referred to as the 'femi-nazi' movement, which has essentially taken hold of the entire Democratic party and leftist movement. Radical leftist feminism focuses on villainizing males at every single opportunity in life. The left now seems to believe that being male is enough reason to consider a person evil. Males are guilty by default.

The plan is simple and accomplishes two critical missions at once:

1)   Turn (up to) 100% of Americans against their gender counterparts
2)   Destroy the nuclear family

Will it work?
This new super-radical brand of man-hating feminism has spread throughout the political class and Hollywood, augmented by the recent 'Me Too' movement. Many women and a few men throughout the US seem to have accepted toxic masculinity as a legitimate concept. More importantly, some large companies have jumped onto the toxic masculinity bandwagon, perhaps in an effort to appear 'woke' or pro-social-justice to potential consumers and/or to ensure that the radical leftist mob passes over (like the story of Passover) them when they seek to destroy all major companies that do not engage in their radical activism. Gillette was the latest company to join the movement, and the response to their YouTube short[40] has been overwhelmingly negative (631,000 downvotes to 251,000 upvotes at the time of this writing). Only time will tell how successful the left's mission (to turn men into second-class citizens?) will be. Fortunately, good parents still do exist and will continue to teach their children that males are not evil just because they are male….at least until being male becomes illegal.

Bait and pushback
Of course, another way of looking at this well-thought out effort is that it could be bait. The radical left may be intentionally pushing against men in order to make men play defense and make themselves appear foolish, radical, or "hyper-masculine". If this is the short-term goal of the movement, it is a very simple and easy one to achieve. All they need to do is continue calling men evil and flirtatious, inappropriate and reckless, and when men become defensive and claim that they are not reckless and violent, they can respond with a 'GOTCHA!' by proving that men are responsible for nearly all violent crime and that men are by nature more reckless.

Utilization of Half-truths
This brings us to perhaps the most significant reason that this movement is seeing success. It is based on scientific facts; men are, by their very nature, more aggressive and reckless. I don't deny this and few men would. The movement takes this genetic fact - one which men cannot be changed - and they take it a massive step further. The movement asserts that men are naturally aggressive, reckless, and therefore, we are all EVIL. Since the movement's message does begin with a truth, it is understandable how some naive (read: 'woke') millennials could fall for it. What

the feminazis don't mention is that all of society (women included) benefits from men having the genetic characteristics[41] that their creator/nature gave them. The majority of military personnel in combat are male. The majority of EMTs, paramedics, and firefighters are male. Males are biologically required in order to have children, so, simply put, the human race would go extinct in one generation without males. This may seem obvious to some, but it seems that ultra-radical feminists get so wrapped up in their hatred for men that they forget how much they really do need men (assuming that they identify with the human race).

Hypocrisy

As we touched upon earlier, the entire message of the feminist movement has become that 'men are horrible creatures who should be shamed and violently punished[42]'. At the same time, the leftist feminist/LGBT message is that there are literally no differences between men and women. Additional hypocrisy within this ridiculous movement involves companies lecturing men about objectifying women while simultaneously objectifying women[43]. Additionally, if hateful feminist companies like Gillette really support equality, they will soon release a video lecturing women on 'toxic femininity', wherein women murder babies, smoke and drink while pregnant, make up false rape allegations, convince boys to commit suicide, etc. If they do not produce this video, they are not in favor of equality, they are just sexist towards men.

Where does this leave us?

The anti-male and anti-freedom movements, which are very closely related, present another compelling reason for separation and independence. States like NY, NJ, and CA will continue to radicalize into communist states and those who seek freedom and true equality will continue to push back. If independence movements (like the ones in New Hampshire, Texas, California, and Washington State) are impeded, violence within this divided nation is inevitable. I simply propose that those of you in NYC and NJ - or even the whole US - want to perpetually assault freedom, whites, males, and all those who don't partake of your radical agenda, go right ahead. Just let us keep New Hampshire.

<u>**Police Vs. Schutzstaffel: Is There A Link?**</u>

In light of the increasingly frequent comparison between modern American police and German law enforcement officers from the 1930s, we figured that we should compare the two to prove that modern American police are nothing like the evil Schutzstaffel (AKA Nazis).

Surveillance

The German government in the 1930s had various forms of surveillance and multiple types of police. German citizens were afraid to speak openly with people, for fear that they might be part of the Gestapo or another Nazi police officer[44]. Eric. A. Johnson compared them to the omnipresent 'Thought Police' from the book '1984': " First appearing in Berlin in April 1933, when Hitler had been in power for only three months, the Gestapo shortly thereafter established large central posts in Germany's major cities and smaller outposts in the rest of Germany's communities. Allegedly endowed with a huge army of specially trained agents and spies and employing advanced technical means of surveillance, the Gestapo, like the "thought police" of George Orwell's terrifying postwar novel 1984, had more than sufficient means to keep close tabs at all times on all citizens—from Jews, Communists, and other "enemies" of the regime to the most insignificant members of German society."

In America, however, we have the 4th Amendment, which prevents law enforcement or any other government official from spying on us or searching our property without due process and/or a warrant from a judge. Local police[45] departments and the US government do not have mass surveillance[46] programs, nor do any states in the nation. Police allow our private lives[47] to remain private and they do not intrude into our personal space and they don't interfere with our personal decisions. Local police departments in the US would never even consider automatically photographing and tracking[48] every license plate, nor would they implement red light cameras[49] or speed cameras[50] just to spy on, control, and extort innocent people.

Due Process & Violence

German police were authorized and encouraged to initiate violence against those who did not obey the law. The tyrants in charge, including Hitler did not grant the German citizens due process. In the US, we have due process, and police cannot do anything to harm any individual because police only encounter individuals who have yet to be convicted in court. Police never see criminals, only suspects, because every American is innocent[51] until proven[52] guilty. Only judges can sentence individuals to be punished, because our Constitution guarantees due process. Police who do hurt[53] or kill[54] civilians are punished harshly. Simply put, American cops cannot get away with murder[55] like the Nazis[56] did. And American cops certainly cannot get away with rape[57,58,59,60].

Conscience

The Schutzstaffel generally obeyed orders and could not get away with disobeying orders from Adolf Hitler or the Nazi leaders. During the Nuremberg trials after WW2, Nazi officials defended themselves by claiming that they were **'just obeying orders'** from their superiors. In America, police are not obligated to follow unconstitutional or immoral orders, and police in America[61] never violate the US Constitution. In the US, the Nuremberg Defense[62] is never used[63] by police.

Protection of civilians

The Nazis don't seem to be known for protecting German citizens from dangers. Though the Nazi Party did use propaganda to turn the populace against the Jews and other minorities and convince them that the Jews were such a threat that they must be removed from society, protection was not their primary function. The primary job of Nazi was to control and terrorize people, especially those who their leaders hated. In the US, however, our cops protect those who cannot protect themselves[64]. When Americans are afraid, we call the police[65]. And they always help us and keep us safe. In fact, the Supreme Court of the US has made an important ruling[66] on the obligation of police to *protect* people. Many government-run schools in the US have amazing[67] police officers in the school[68] at all times. Without police, we would be so unsafe!

Worship of police & government

Similar to many socialist and communist regimes, the citizenry in Germany circa 1930 became brainwashed into adoring Hitler[69] and the Nazis in a cult-like fashion. Indeed, being a Nazi officer was well respected and supported very strongly by the Aryan Germans. The government also used propaganda[70] to normalize their actions and to make the citizens love them. In the US, citizens are smart enough to avoid falling for that sort of manipulation. We do not worship police[71] or politicians and we hold them accountable when they violate[72] the law or when they hurt someone.

Stop & Frisk
German officials could stop and search citizens whenever they wanted, without needing any specific reason. Americans are protected from such searches and seizures by the 4th amendment to our Constitution. Unlike the SS, American police cannot 'stop & frisk[73]' random people just because they feel like it. Our police certainly would not coerce innocent people into providing cheek swabs[74] just to 'have their DNA samples on file'.

Corruption
The Nazi officers and the Nazi Party in general were surely corrupt. They seized control of the German government and turned it into a murderous, controlling, dictatorship. In the US, police officers are not corrupt[75] and police and government leaders[76] are never involved in corrupt[77] activity.

God bless the USA and God bless our police!

The Union Cannot Survive

From an early age, American children are inaccurately taught that the United States of America is one big, happy nation and that keeping the union together is the ultimate American priority. Many teachers impress upon children the idea that, while individual states retain their own identities, cultures, laws, accents, industries, and appearances, those differences comprise the diversity that makes America so strong. As children grow up and turn into voters, they often rationalize the relatively futile[78] practice of voting against perpetual opposition by insisting that *'in THIS election, we just need to elect the right people to represent us in DC, and then we can really fix this nation!'* Ironically, most Americans would probably agree that "insanity is doing the same thing over and over and expecting different results".

Though the United States is actually a federation of many different peoples, norms, and cultures, the education that children in the US receive is controlled by one central government. This government trains students to be obedient (and even to love, respect, defend) the government while neglecting to teach them about the merits of independence, individualism, personal liberty, skepticism, and decentralization.

One of the greatest grievances one can have against the government's education system may be their neglecting to teach children that 'State' is and always has been a synonym with 'Country'. Nearly every American adult to whom I've mentioned this was shocked to hear it. While it may seem like irrelevant semantics to some, this distinction is extremely important. The founders created the US Constitution with careful deliberation, debate, and foresight, and the document created a very weak, small central government, with the intent that each State would continue to govern itself in almost every aspect of life.

The US government was hardly even supposed[79] to be a government, rather it was formed as a weak union among all of the states, essentially for the purposes of having generals who could lead one US military and arbiters who could settle disputes regarding interstate trade. The US government has grown to become much more than a weak union; it is now an omnipotent monstrosity that creates billions of laws, collects $3 trillion and spends $4 trillion a year, and employs millions of agents who further abuse Americans.

How do individual Americans feel about the central government?

Let's review the basics of civics for those who are not yet familiar with the US governmental structure. The central government is comprised of:

The **executive** branch, which includes the president, his cabinet, and most of the 400+ federal agencies.

The **legislative** branch (Congress), which includes the US House and US Senate. The House is composed of 435 Representatives who are elected by districts in each State depending on the population. The Senate is composed of 2 Senators from each State.

The **judicial** branch, which comprises the Supreme Court and all federal courts.

The US House and Senate are thought by naive voters to represent the American people extremely well. Elections seem much better in theory than their results ever seem to be, though. Would you believe that nearly every American disapproves of Congress? The US House elects a Speaker, who controls the House. 'Americans' hate her, and they always seem to hate the Speaker. The US Senate's majority and minority parties (currently Republicans and Democrats) each elect a leader. The two current leaders - McConnell and Schumer - are hated by nearly every human in 'America'. The president always seems to be hated by Americans, and even their general election opponent seems to be hated[80] by their own party!

In a randomized, scientific poll of 134,000 Americans, Civiqs found that 57% of people believe that the 'nation' is headed in the wrong direction, while only 36%[81] believed that America is headed in the right direction. Learning about all of the surveys on their site may help you realize that 'Americans' are beyond divided and unsatisfied with their lives under one central government. Though the majority of them do not realize it yet, nearly all Americans want their government to be much more local and accountable to them than the current government in Washington DC. Every time the government harms us, more people ask themselves: Maybe a few out of touch leaders can't truly represent[82] 330 million individual people who live in 50 individual nations?

In addition to Americans being thoroughly disgusted with every new wave of leaders in Washington DC, the ever-increasing number of federal agencies (currently over 400), and the ever-increasing federal spending and debt, individuals in different States really are much too different to live peacefully as one nation.

How drastically do individuals differ on major issues?

Abortion
The right to abort a fetus vs. the protection of the lives of babies has been an extremely intense debate among Americans for at least a few decades, and for good reason. In recent weeks, a few conservative States have passed laws that restrict abortions[83] much more than their previous laws did. The outcry from pro-abortion individuals in those conservative States and in progressive States has been tremendous[84]. Due to the United States government taking ultimate control of abortion laws (generally via the Supreme Court) which determine how over 300 million unique individuals in 50 distinct States could legally navigate a complex issue, even the most progressive, pro-abortion states are forced to worry that the Supreme Court may revisit the issue. If the five "Republican" judges rule that the Alabama law is legal, abortion could be totally banned in all 50 States. The only way that the Democratic States would then be able to continue to allow women to have abortions would be to separate (secede) from the United States.

Conversely, if the Court rules that abortion ought to be legal, conservative States would likely have to leave the union in order to protect the lives of babies. Abortion is extremely complicated and involves religion, medicine, ethics, finances, law, and so much more. What is not complicated is that if States do not want to be governed by a few old, out-of-touch lawyers who live in DC, their only solution may be to peacefully exit the union, as the UK recently decided to do.

Gun Control
The debate whether firearms should be banned, heavily regulated, weakly regulated, or totally unregulated[85] (which is what the founders supported) is another one of the many polarizing issues tearing the union apart. States like New Hampshire, Wyoming, Alaska, Arizona, and a few others have essentially no restrictions on firearms. In those states, the only restrictions on firearms are the federal laws, such as the NICS background check, the irrelevant prohibition of automatic firearms and suppressors, and short barreled rifle restrictions. Those States are consistently ranked as the safest in the nation because criminals are forced to consider that any random person may be armed. Sixteen US States currently do not force citizens to obtain permits before carrying firearms. Wyoming citizens love their firearms freedoms and likely don't care whether NYC[86] considers all guns illegal (which happens to be the case). However, Wyoming does not want to be forced to give up its firearms because the few politicians who run the central government want all US citizens to be disarmed, which would make any potential rebellion nearly impossible. As federal politicians pass laws that chip away at gun rights utilizing convoluted and inconspicuous methods, all Americans will continually lose more gun rights, until the entire 'America' has the same gun laws as NYC.

In this national poll[87], 53% of Americans favored stricter gun control, while 41% opposed stricter gun control. Looking at respondents in each political party paints a clear picture of this true distinction (Civiqs does not have a breakdown of each State for this survey). It is very obvious that individuals in conservatives States favor the freedom to own weapons[88] and the individuals in progressive States want weapons to remain only in the hands of government/police officials. Currently, both sides are working against the monstrosity referred to as the federal government, so neither side is happy, and neither side can move the needle much in their favor.

Conservative States have a gun culture in which 8 year olds are often given their first .22 caliber rifle for Christmas. Progressive States have the opposite cultural view of firearms. From childhood, leftist parents and schools teach their children that firearms are bad and belong only in the hands of government agents.

California, Oregon, and Washington could attain their gun-control dreams by peacefully exiting the union, either individually or as a nation or union of their own. Massachusetts, Vermont, Rhode Island, Connecticut, New York, New

Jersey, Maryland, Delaware, and Virginia could exit the union and decide for themselves whether to remain alone for a while or whether to seek a union with one or more other States. Conversely or additionally, Wyoming, Utah, Idaho, Montana, the Dakotas, Nebraska, Missouri, Kansas, Oklahoma, and maybe Texas ought to consider ditching the US government and taking freedom back for themselves. Ideally, every one of the 50 States would leave the union and tell the DC folks to go to hell.

Education

Individuals in each of the 50 States have very different wishes for how to educate their children. Unfortunately for all of them, a few elite politicians, judges, and bureaucrats in DC control education throughout 'America'. There are over 150 federal dictates that control how American parents educate their children. Though it may seem like State and local laws regarding education do exist, they are impotent. Firstly, school districts and States can only control education within the federal scope of allowable conduct. Secondly, the federal government bullies smaller governments when they make decisions that do not please the federal politicians. Thirdly, even the laws, regulations, and standards that seem to come from the State or school districts are very often influenced by federal grants[89].

Progressive States seem to be increasingly inviting drag-queens[90] to conduct storytime with young children, encouraging[91] children to transition to the opposite gender, and they are allowing increasing amounts of biological males[92] to compete in female athletics simply because they claim to 'identify' as females. In response to this massive change in athletic competition between the two genders, the United State House of Representatives recently passed the 'Equality Act[93]', which would force every school in the US to allow boys to compete with girls in every sport if they 'identify' as girls, should the bill become law. The bill would also effect massive expansions in the Civil Rights Act, taking away many more liberties from Americans under the guise of 'opposing discrimination'.

Furthermore, individuals in States like Utah would likely want their religion (Christianity) to be the foundation for their education system. Progressive States like California, New York, and New Jersey are composed of parents who want religion (especially Christianity) to be totally absent from schools. Parents in different States may also have unique approaches to vocational education, degrees, standards, athletics, and more. The only way to break free from outside, homogenous, harmful control over our children's education must involve cutting ties with the DC politicians for good.

Drug Regulation

Have you spoken to anyone about cannabis recently? It seems that very few Americans believe that it should be illegal, doesn't it? According to national scientific surveys, only 24%[94] of Americans believe that it should be illegal. Yet, the unaccountable, unresponsive, out of touch central government still considers cannabis to be a schedule 1 controlled substance, which is the strictest, most illegal, dangerous category that the US government has. This is no surprise to those who understand how difficult it is to hold elite, powerful, apathetic, corrupt millionaires accountable when they live far away and literally own you.

Thirty-three States currently allow their citizens to use cannabis medicinally, and nine States allow its use recreationally. This act of defiance against the federal government may seem to be cause for optimism. While nullification of federal cannabis laws by some States may lead some to believe that States could retain some autonomy in this centrally-controlled, post-constitutional climate, federal politicians could decide at any moment to cut off funding/grants (paid for by federal taxes) to any State that does not enforce the federal prohibition of cannabis. Indeed, even Colorado's incredible drug-legalization momentum could be thwarted by President Trump in an instant.

Federal politicians utilize nearly every one of their 400+ federal agencies to control and abuse individuals. The Food and Drug Administration is one of those agencies. Now that you are aware of the 'representation-accountability ratio' (local governments are more accountable than massive, faraway governments) it should come as no surprise that the FDA[95] is one of the strictest drug approval agencies in the world. It is also extremely corrupt, as I point out in an article[96] about the EpiPen scandal and as many others often prove. Simply put, politicians and regulators often utilize the FDA to approve drugs that benefit themselves and their friends and deny drugs that would harm their businesses. The agency also regulates food so strictly that even your cherry pie[97] is subject to numerous federal laws. And you are forced by the threat of violence and criminal prosecution to pay more than $5,000,000,000[98] ($5 billion) every year to fund this abusive agency.

We could take the power back from politicians like Trump, Schumer, McConnell, Pelosi, and Feinstein by simply cutting ties with them - much like we would all recommend to our loved ones when they are in relationships with controlling and abusive partners.

Immigration

Perhaps no greater division exists between conservatives and progressives than their differing opinions on illegal immigration and border security. Conservatives elected Trump despite barely trusting him, because he seemed much tougher than Clinton on illegal immigration and because he made a border wall a primary campaign issue. Now that Trump is a politician, it's no surprise that he has largely failed to deliver on his promise to quickly construct a 'big, beautiful wall' along the southern border of the US. Still, conservatives and progressive throughout the US who are forced to live under the same set of immigration laws continue to resent each other. Once in a while, someone wonders "Couldn't some States invite illegal immigrants while others reject them? Why can't individuals in each State consider whether their State should have a wall around it? What happened to the will of the people?"

Since federal politicians control immigration policy and redistribute the wealth of all Americans, each of us is forced to shoulder the financial burden of illegal immigrants pouring into the US, which currently costs over $54 billion per year[99], according to Heritage.org.

Surveys and common knowledge demonstrate the differences of opinion that each State has towards immigration policy. Among Californians, 68% of individuals[100] **oppose** having a border wall for their nation. On the flip side, 67% of individuals in Wyoming[101] **support** having a border wall around their nation. Of course, such polar differences on issues concerning national security, socialism, and human rights cannot be reconciled while being forced to live under one policy. The only scenario in which people in each State could be satisfied and feel safe involves peaceful separation from the corrupt, controlling, out-of-touch central government.

Why Conservatives Should Support Secession

If you are a conservative who hopes that 'America will survive', take a look at a poll[102] which shows that 46% of Americans not only love Obamacare but want to expand it. Only 39% of those surveyed wanted the massive, strict healthcare doctrine to be repealed. Unfortunately for those who support gun rights, there are many strict federal gun laws, yet 53% of Americans want even stricter gun control, while only 41% support[103] more firearms freedom. Optimistic conservatives might also be disappointed to learn that the next generation (18-29 year olds) have a negative view of capitalism[104]. You may only know middle America, but the increasing coastal and city populations are increasingly composed of active young voters who are progressive, pro-LGBT, authoritarian socialists who wish to force their big-government policies onto you. If you do not want to be forced to live increasingly similar lifestyles to theirs, congratulations - you support State independence!

Why Progressives Should Support Secession

If you are a progressive who believes that the whole 'America' would be happy as 'one united socialist nation', you would be disappointed to learn that when it comes to making meaningful decisions (like choosing a State to live in) Americans are fleeing[105] progressive states and moving to conservative/low tax states. The US Census next year will count the number of Americans in each State, which is likely the primary reason that Democrats are pushing[106] so hard to begin counting illegal aliens in the next Census. If they do not change the rules, California, New York, New Jersey, and Illinois may lose congressional seats due to their massive population losses since the 2010 Census. Additionally, only 41% of Americans[107] approve of the Democratic party. Not everyone in 'America' is 'just like you'. Other than the few million Americans in the large cities, nearly every American is actually pretty much your complete opposite. Around half of the people in America are religious, gun-toting, conservative capitalists. If you do not want to be forced to live increasingly similar lifestyles to theirs, congratulations - you support State independence!

Both sides of the political spectrum could truly be satisfied simply by living among like-minded people. Why would you remain in a hostile environment where you believe your culture is under perpetual attack?

Secession Vs. Slavery

Some foolish individuals, including conservatives, mistakenly believe that because slavery was claimed by the winner of the civil war (the strong central government) to be a major issue contributing to the Confederacy's desire to secede, all future attempts by States on Earth to peacefully divorce from oppressive and/or corrupt strong central governments must be due to the desire to bring back slavery. Of course, this is a ridiculous notion, especially because the pro-freedom States would secede in order to respect property rights and individual freedom **more** than the current government does.

The Military Issue

One of the most difficult realities for people to reconcile when considering the inevitable fracture of the Union is the military. While it is true that the US military is by far the strongest force on the planet (possibly by a factor of a few hundred) and that its strength is related to its drawing from 50 powerful States, it is hardly true that independence would change that. Even if the central government were to be entirely dissolved, nothing is to stop Governors (commanders-in-chief of each State National Guard, even according to current laws) from working together with other State militaries on a perpetual or occasional basis. Currently, the US military may work together with over 100 other militaries in 150 foreign nations[108] due to their massive amounts of military operations. The militaries that they work with speak different languages and train differently because they are literally from other parts of the world. It would be infinitely easier for State militaries in post-union America to work together. Keep in mind that once American soldiers stop intervening in every single issue on Earth, very little has to be done militarily. All we need to do is play defense.

The Trade Issue

Without a corrupt, oppressive central government creating and enforcing millions of laws restricting free trade, interstate commerce would prosper enormously. Businesses and consumers would save billions or maybe even trillions of dollars annually without the federal government controlling interstate trade. In the event of a conflict between individuals or businesses from different States, courts, contracts, and arbitrations could settle disputes just like they do now.

In addition to the above issues, the numerous cultures among the 50 States surely differ dramatically on many more policies. The founders cited 'irreconcilable differences' in their grievances to the British King when they declared independence from his tyranny. In 2019, there are much more extreme and irreconcilable differences between the States and the US government that are much more tyrannical than the British government ever was. The solution is simple: Each of us must work to empower our States to peacefully divorce themselves from the abusive authoritarian politicians who are destroying our lives. Once we are governed only by local and accountable officials, we will see a rapid increase in the amount of freedom and the quality of life that we all enjoy.

Incredible Democrat Hypocrisy On Double Taxation

In response to President Trump and the congressional Republicans passing a comprehensive tax reform bill, Democrat leaders have issued strong statements condemning the new changes in the US federal tax code. It must be stressed that the new tax plan remains convoluted, manipulative, and deceitful. That said, the Democrats legislate in that same manner, and the GOP tax bill did improve the tax code in a few crucial ways:

1.   It repealed the horrifically unpopular individual mandate - a part of Obamacare that punished Americans who did not have health insurance by forcing them to pay a fine.
2.   The bill doubles the child tax credit from $1,000 per child to $2,000 per child, decreasing taxes for millions of middle-class families.
3.   The rate at which businesses are taxed was decreased from 35% to 21%.This has allowed companies to keep more money, which they have passed on to their employees.
4.   Of the 7 tax brackets, 5 of them decreased with the TCJA. This means that middle class earners received a substantial tax cut.
5.   The bill placed a cap on how much money could be deducted from federally taxable income, forcing the rich to 'pay their fair share', as Senator Bernie Sanders has been pleading for years.
6.   The bill increased the bottom threshold for the 'death tax'. This allowed family businesses and individuals to pass up to $11 million of their worth to their children without the federal government stealing 40%[109] of the individual's or business' worth.

I have little interest in writing a tax policy article. It's been done from every angle (surely by journalists and tax experts much wiser than me) ad infinitum. I hardly even care to mention how foolish many of the Democrat leaders have made themselves appear when they held press conferences condemning the GOP for *"hurting the middle class," despite* this being the biggest tax cut for the middle class in my lifetime (yes, I got a large tax cut). No, none of that is what inspired me to jump back into the politics of the US, the nation that I have largely given up on. What honestly got me fired up enough to join in on the discussion relating to the most complex tax code in the history of the universe is that liberals in high-income-tax and socialist states like Governor Cuomo of NY repeatedly speak about this bill and make insane and deceitful statements, such as:

"This is like paying taxes on your taxes" and **"There's never been a double taxation in the history of our nation"** and "They then eliminate the deductibility of state and local taxes[110]".

Many national leaders of the Democrat Party and the socialist movement embarrassed themselves when discussing the tax reform bill for the sole purpose of using opposition to Republican policy as a means to increase donations and interest in the failing party:

Senator Elizabeth Warren made at least two insane comments on the bill:

"This corruption is hollowing out America's middle class & tearing down our democracy."

"It's not tax reform. It's a heist. A heist that steals from millions of middle-class families and hands that money over to the wealthy."

Senator Mark Warner's comment was the most exaggerated statement in the history of humanity!

"This is the worst piece of legislation we have passed since I arrived in the Senate."

Democrat Senate leader Chuck Schumer made his case for the 'most ridiculous statements ever award' with these two gems:

"It's a bill that's cutting taxes on the wealthiest Americans..."

"Americans prefer DEMOCRATS to REPUBLICANS on taxes…"

Democrat House Leader, Nancy Pelosi tweeted this:

"Shamefully, Republicans were cheering against the children as they rob from their future and ransack the middle class to reward the rich #GOPTaxScam"

These politicians' statements could hardly be further from the truth. But Andrew Cuomo's stupidity goes far beyond what we generally see from partisan political statements. The socialist New York governor has been doing his best to convince New Yorkers that Trump is completely abolishing[111] the deduction for state and local income tax and property tax. This is absolutely false. To keep things very simple, taxpayers have been able to deduct their state, local, and property taxes from their gross taxable income, allowing them to pay federal taxes on a slightly lower sum of their income. This saves middle class Americans a few hundred dollars a year on their federal income taxes. The GOP tax bill does not change that! The Tax Cuts & Jobs Act forces the wealthy to pay federal taxes without taking advantage of this 'tax code loophole'. Before 2018, liberals in NY earning $50,000 a year might be forced to pay around $10,000 in combined state/local/property taxes and then they would pay their federal taxes as if they only earned $40,000 that year. This means that they had a **tax deduction** of $10,000. Now let's take a look at the 'evil rich people' living in states like NY: Imagine that Mr. Richie McFascist earned a million dollars a year. Since he would be taxed 100-200k by NY, he might only pay federal taxes on 800k! Once he uses all of his other tricks and cheats, he might end up paying federal taxes on only a tiny sum of money, meaning that the federal government gets the short end of the stick. The new plan limits that deduction to $10,000. This means that it really only applies to individuals who earn more than around $100k a year and/or own a very expensive home and pay a high property tax. Those in the middle class will absolutely enjoy a significant tax cut. Those with children will keep an even larger amount of their money this year, due to the TCJA giving people an extra $1,000 for each child they have.

In what may go down in history as one of the great political lies (I know, there's infinite competition) Cuomo remarked; **"There's never been a double taxation in the history of our nation".** There actually has been and still is double taxation, you buffoon. Like most actual fascism[112] that has occurred in US history, this tale begins with Democrat hero, FDR. President Roosevelt created the Social Security Administration. In short, it's this great program that entails stealing income from people based on the false promise that they will get it back when the government decides that they are old enough to use it responsibly, which at the time was 65 years old. Later, this increased to 66 years old. And then 67. In a case of incredible irony, the US government was proven to be the irresponsible party when the public learned that they lost the money in the fund, causing social security to be insolvent. President Reagan and the Democrat House decided in 1984 that American seniors must **pay taxes** on their social security checks - just like they do on income. This is obviously ridiculous and fascist because those seniors likely paid millions of dollars into SS throughout their entire lives via **taxation**.

That is the reason that I cannot bear to hear bastards like Cuomo[113] lie about being 'taxed on taxes'. Cuomo: Until you stop taxing your citizens[114] into submission and until you stop worshipping FDR, and until you repeal the social security double-tax, you need to shut up about 'taxes on taxes'.

While the GOP did little to uncomplicate the 70,000+ page federal tax code, they absolutely did decrease the income tax burden for the middle class of the US (as well as the upper and lower classes). The last people who have a leg to stand on when criticizing the changes made to the tax code are Democrat politicians. If authoritarian socialists do wish to criticize the changes, they would be wiser to be truthful and to advocate for less, not more money to be taken forcibly from the middle class. Democrats like Governor Cuomo can put his money where his mouth is by getting to work on cutting taxes for the struggling workers in New York, lest he empowers his Libertarian opponent Larry Sharpe with even more fuel.

<u>Dear Tailgater</u>

After leaving work today, I drove home using my usual route. As I've resolved to do ever since receiving a hefty speeding ticket (on this very road), I obeyed the posted speed limit for every road I drove on. On this road, it was 35 MPH, though the normal flow of traffic was usually around 50-60 MPH. When I obey the posted speed limit, drivers often tailgate me and they usually seem pretty frustrated that I'm forcing them to actually obey the law - the same law that they surely support with their votes and their 'I support my local police' law signs. Today, my tailgater was a middle-aged woman who seemed particularly annoyed at me for obeying the law. She was following within around a foot of my car at times, and she continually made aggressive hand gestures. When I finally turned off of the main road just to begin writing this article on my phone, she turned in my direction and clearly mouthed some angry words at me.

The tailgater must have thought that I was driving so ridiculously slowly either to annoy her or because I was incompetent. Of course, I was just behaving like a 'law abiding citizen[115]', as I've been told by so many people that I must do.

Months ago, I ordered stickers in an effort to solve this exact dilemma. The stickers read:

Am I driving too slow? Rethink speed limit laws!

That was all the sticker had space for while still being legible. I put the sticker on my car, but I've since removed it, for fear of making cops even more upset when they pull me over. I also don't think that a few words on a sticker could really explain my thoughts on speed limits to frustrated tailgaters. So, I decided to write this article.

For clarity, the relevant state laws regarding speeding New Hampshire appear to be:

Maximum speed law:

According to section 265:60 (I) of New Hampshire vehicle code, "A person shall not drive a vehicle at a speed greater than is reasonable and prudent under the conditions, having regard to the actual and potential hazards then existing."

Minimum speed law:

Sections 265:64 (I) and 265:16 (II) state:

"A person shall not drive a vehicle at such a slow speed as to impede the normal and reasonable movement of traffic."

Of course, the above laws are contradictory; obeying the speed limit means driving slowly enough to impede normal traffic quite often - as my above story illustrates.

If you are one of the drivers in New Hampshire (or anywhere else in the world) who believes that some speed limits are much slower than the safe, normal flow of traffic on a given road, you have two options:

1) Continue to be a hypocrite by violating the law while also preaching about how people 'must obey the law' no matter how they feel about it and by voting for increasingly strict speed limits and traffic enforcement. Roughly 100% of people fall into this category, according to a Purdue University study[116].

2) You can email, call, and pester New Hampshire's State Representatives, Senators, Governor, DOT, and anyone else who may have influence over our speed limits and traffic enforcement, forcing them to change the laws.

As we explain in many articles[117], traffic laws and enforcement throughout the US have become a joke. Nearly every driver knows that traffic enforcement has become primarily about control and revenue and not about safety. If politicians and cops cared about safety, this article[118] about police changing their ways would not be considered satire.

Dear Tailgater,

I know that you are frustrated. I also want to drive faster. I have been driving at speeds two to three times many posted speed limits for years while remaining totally safe and responsible. I have been teaching people how to drive emergency vehicles since 2012. I remain one of the most safe and conservative drivers you might ever meet. I have driven hundreds of thousands of miles, in 40 states, and in every driving condition imaginable. Nobody has ever been hurt as a result of my driving. I could safely drive 80 on that highway despite its 35 MPH speed limit. Believe me, I wish I could. I am one of the busiest and most efficient individuals I know. I have places to be, just like you do.

However, until you and all others like you begin to demand that our legislators either increase or repeal speed limits or end traffic enforcement for the crime of 'speeding', I will continue to obey the law. I simply cannot continue to pay hundreds of dollars in fines for the crime of violating the law. Losing hundreds of dollars could mean that the mortgage doesn't get paid or that my family has to go into debt. We cannot take that risk. I am sure that you could understand this thought process.

So, I will continue to obey all posted speed limits. This will mean that I will drive much too slowly until the laws in New Hampshire are changed. Please be careful when driving and do not follow too closely. If I would have tapped my brakes today, my tailgater would have crashed into me. I apologize for the inconvenience and I hope that this can motivate you to get politically involved in order to hold our legislators accountable to the will of the people.

P.S. This tool[119] can help you find your Representative(s) and your Senator can be found here[120]. Governor Sununu can be contacted here[121]. The DOT can be contacted here[122]. It's not yet clear who exactly controls which speed limits. I am happy to help you connect with any legislator if needed. I've already contacted them all.

<u>Socialist Bill Gives Politicians More Control Over Restaurants</u>

A bill proposed by four Democrats and two Republicans would give the government (read: politicians and bureaucrats) another degree of control over restaurants. In addition to requiring business licenses for every business and the many other burdensome, unnecessary, and authoritarian regulations, politicians are hellbent on taking control of restaurants by utilizing the concept of 'safety' and 'public health', as they often do. If the government should have the authority to micromanage restaurants in the name of 'the health of their customers', maybe this bill doesn't actually go far enough.

House Bill 1102[123] forces all *"food service establishments to establish food allergy awareness procedures."* The bill explains that the new requirements would make it a crime for restaurant owners to neglect to:

"(a) Include on all menus and menu boards a notice to customers of the customer's obligation to inform the server of his or her food allergies.

(b) Have a person in charge during all hours of operation trained and certified as a food protection manager by a program approved by the department which includes training regarding food allergens. Such person shall ensure that employees are properly informed of food safety issues, including awareness of food allergies, as it is related to the employees' assigned duties."

Violating this new law could result in **"the suspension or revocation of a food service establishment license."**

Of course, following these new requirements would force - and I do mean force using the threat of violence - restaurant owners to change all of their menus. This includes their printed menus, their TV screens in the restaurant, and their online menus to reflect the new potential allergens, which may have to include every substance. This would cost time and money. And the rule of economics states that the more costly it is for a business to bring a product and/or service to the customer, the more expensive it becomes for the customer. Additionally, the bill would force entrepreneurs to train or hire an employee who would need to be certified by the government as a 'food protection manager'. This person would also have to spend time training employees on allergies, which would cost the business more time and money. It is unclear which allergies the government is looking to force restaurant employees to learn about. It could be the common ones like peanuts and shellfish, it could be all allergies, and it could mean anything else the government decides. People can be allergic to anything. One thing is for sure, though: Your restaurant bill would increase substantially if HB1102 becomes law.

How do people currently survive the experience of eating out? Don't many people actually enjoy eating out? How do they know which restaurants are good and which will kill them by way of allergies or other health risks?

Anyone with a brain understands that people - especially as consumers - are quite intelligent. They regularly learn about restaurants and all businesses using Google, Yelp, Facebook, other sites, and word of mouth before ever giving their money to a business. This affords people the ultimate freedom to choose where to spend their money, it holds businesses extremely accountable to their customers, and it keeps prices low and quality and customer service high. The authors of HB1102 believe that you are ignorant, Google doesn't work, and that restaurant owners are trying to kill you (and here I thought that restaurants wanted repeat customers, not dead customers). If that is the case, their bill does not go far enough to protect individuals from themselves. Here is a proposal to make the bill more effective:

Being that heart disease is the #1 cause of death in the United States and in New Hampshire, and being that restaurant foods contribute significantly to heart disease, all food service establishments shall:

a) Include on all menus and menu boards a notice to customers of the customer's obligation to inform the server of his or her diseases, illnesses, medications, and other injuries, conditions, and special dietary needs.

(b) Have a person in charge during all hours of operation trained and certified as a heart health manager' by a program approved by the department which includes training regarding heart disease, hypertension, and health food choices. Such person shall ensure that employees are properly informed of food safety issues, including awareness of heart disease, as it is related to the employees' assigned duties."

c) All employees shall be trained in CPR and hold current AHA or equivalent CPR certifications.

d) All employees shall be trained and certified by the department to recognize the symptoms of a heart attack, stroke, and pulmonary embolism.

e) Include an AED on their property and train all employees in its use. In the event that a severe heart attack or other condition causes sudden cardiac arrest, rapid recognition, CPR, and use of an AED have been shown to dramatically increase the rate of survival.

f) No single meal offered by the establishment shall contain more than half of the FDA recommended daily allowance of sodium[124]. As of 2019, the total daily recommended amount of sodium is 2,300mg.

While heart disease does not often kill restaurant patrons as quickly as severe allergies, it is so much more common and kills so many more people than any other disease, injury, or condition, that politicians who are consistent in their desire to 'protect' people from themselves should seriously consider adding the heart disease section to their new bill. If people should not have the freedom to choose what to put into their bodies and if entrepreneurs must be micromanaged by the government, this is the next logical step. Or politicians can simply ban cheeseburgers, alcohol, smoking, cholesterol, sugar, salt, and every other unhealthy substance[125] that free people enjoy.

Lose A Gun And Go To Jail

A bill proposed by four Democratic Senators could send peaceful gun owners to prison for a year and fine them $2,000.

Senate Bill 719[126] appears on the surface to be a common-sense bill. In fact, this author initially felt ambivalent when glancing at the bill, which simply purports to establish *"procedures for reporting a lost or stolen firearm."* I did not read the full bill, and I doubt many others did, either.

Just a few moments ago, I remembered that I did 'lose' a firearm around a week ago, and I did not report it to the police. Something told me that I should check the bill for specifics and for punishments; tyrants often propose harsh punishments for violating laws created by their authoritarian bills. Here is what I found in the bill's text:

"If such person purposely fails to make such report within the prescribed time period, such person shall be guilty of a class A misdemeanor."

According to New Hampshire law, a class A misdemeanor[127] conviction could result in a year in prison and/or a fine of $2,000 for the defendant. I temporarily could not locate one of my firearms due to moving all of my firearms out of my house in their cases and asking various friends to hold on to them while I ran to a hotel due to a house fire. If this bill were already the law, I would be guilty of a serious crime and I would be facing a year in prison for knowingly failing to report a lost firearm within the prescribed period (which is 3 days). As we settled back into the house after staying in a hotel for two weeks, I located all of my firearms, as I knew I would. If you have ever misplaced or forgotten where you left a firearm, you should strongly oppose this insane bill.

How did the cunning authors of the bill slip this one past so many watchdogs?

In addition to the title/analysis of the bill making it seem benign, the language itself is somewhat misleading:

Any person who fails to make a report required under paragraph I shall be guilty of a violation and shall be fined not more than $100 for a first offense, and shall be guilty of a class B misdemeanor for any subsequent offense. If such person purposely fails to make such report within the prescribed time period, such person shall be guilty of a class A misdemeanor.

Unless you read the final sentence of this section, you might not see a major issue with this bill. Of course, the only difference in the final sentence is the word 'purposefully'. Any prosecutor worth his weight in trash could prove that a person who neglected to report a lost or stolen firearm for three full days did so 'purposefully'. This is one of the many tactics that tyrants use - and that The Liberty Block strives to inform people about.

This bill seems to argue that it is critically important to alert 'the authorities' whenever an individual loses track of something that could be potentially dangerous. Losing a firearm could be dangerous because a person who finds it might hurt someone using the firearm. Considering that New Hampshire citizens own roughly the same amount of firearms as vehicles, car crashes are more likely[128] than firearms to injure and to kill people. As such, this bill should be amended to include the mandatory reporting of the loss or theft of one's car keys.

Another interesting note is that this bill is model legislation[129] from the anti-gun group, 'Giffords Law Center To Prevent Gun Violence'. This further demonstrates how anti-gun the bill's roots are. The website's page on model legislation states that this model bill *"Requires any firearm owner or possessor to report the loss or theft of his or her firearm to law enforcement within 48 hours of the time he or she knew or reasonably should have known of the loss or theft. (*In today's world, even Giffords might be condemned for insulting all non-binary individuals by using such language as "he or she".)

The Senate Judiciary Committee will likely recommend that the whole Senate pass this bill. This vote will take place very soon. Find and email your Senator and tell them to oppose this fascist, authoritarian, anti-freedom, anti-gun bill. If it passes the Senate, we will update you and help you contact your Representatives.

UPDATE: This bill has been killed, thanks to you.

======================

Thank you so much for reading volume 1 of 'Essays on Freedom'. I hope that you enjoyed it! Please visit LibertyBlock.com to read many more articles and to find lots of news and opinion from a pro-freedom perspective. Check out our podcast if you prefer to listen to content. If you enjoyed the book, I would REALLY appreciate it if you could leave a review on Amazon so that other readers like you can find this book, too. Email me at alu.axelman@gmail.com if you have any questions or if you want to discuss any of these articles. Thanks!!!

Endnotes

1. https://www.cnn.com/2017/11/30/us/kate-steinle-murder-trial-verdict/index.html
2. http://www.foxnews.com/us/2018/03/16/kate-steinle-murder-case-explained-from-trumps-comments-to-doj-arrest-warrant.html
3. https://www.youtube.com/watch?v=MdAyn89hFlo
4. https://www.theblaze.com/news/2017/01/09/over-98-of-mass-shootings-occurred-on-gun-free-zones-research-shows
5. http://heyjackass.com
6. http://www.latimes.com/nation/la-na-liang-sentencing-20160419-story.html
7. https://www.theroot.com/10-disgusting-things-joe-arpaio-did-as-sheriff-of-maric-1798459059
8. http://www.miamiherald.com/news/local/crime/article144190724.html
9. https://youtu.be/JTKTfUHfeKM?t=16s
10. http://newyork.cbslocal.com/2017/04/25/nypd-gun-license-bribery-scheme-case/
11. https://www.theroot.com/baltimore-cops-kept-toy-guns-to-plant-just-in-case-they-1822546984
12. https://www.youtube.com/watch?v=hJPVglqR4yM
13. https://www.youtube.com/watch?v=agL59nLBAqk
14. https://youtu.be/X-WJMoxMfm4?t=42s
15. http://www.foxnews.com/us/2018/03/14/teacher-accidentally-fires-gun-in-class-students-injured.html
16. http://www.wlwt.com/article/new-ballpark-foods-for-the-2018-season/19606050
17. http://tribunist.com/news/supreme-court-ruling-police-have-no-duty-to-protect-the-general-public/
18. https://www.cnn.com/2018/03/27/politics/john-paul-stevens-second-amendment/index.html
19. https://abcnews.go.com/Politics/obamas-deportation-policy-numbers/story?id=41715661
20. http://www.latimes.com/politics/la-na-pol-trump-marijuana-20180608-story.html
21. https://www.cnn.com/2018/05/14/politics/sports-betting-ncaa-supreme-court/index.html
22. www.courthousenews.com/justices-gorsuch-and-sotomayor-unlikely-allies-in-police-search-cases/
23. https://smartasset.com/taxes/all-about-child-tax-credits
24. https://www.usatoday.com/story/money/2018/01/26/did-your-company-pay-you-bonus-tax-savings-check-list/1065291001/
25. http://www.kowal.com/?q=How-Many-Federal-Laws-Are-There%3F
26. http://www.nam.org/Data-and-Reports/Cost-of-Federal-Regulations/Federal-Regulation-Executive-Summary.pdf
27. http://thehill.com/homenews/administration/316839-trump-to-sign-order-reducing-regulations
28. https://www.washingtonexaminer.com/trump-kills-16-regulations-for-every-new-one-crushing-2-for-1-goal
29. https://libertyblock.com/a-manchin-of-corruption/
30. http://thehill.com/blogs/pundits-blog/the-administration/312436-confiscator-in-chief-obamas-last-minute-land-grab-an
31. http://www.usdebtclock.org/
32. http://www.chicagotribune.com/news/nationworld/politics/ct-trump-utah-national-monuments-20171204-story.html
33. https://www.washingtonpost.com/world/national-security/sessions-greenlights-police-to-increase-seizures-of-cash-and-property-from-suspected-criminals
34. https://en.wikipedia.org/wiki/Political_appointments_by_Donald_Trump
35. https://www.npr.org/2016/11/29/503797983/carrier-trump-reach-deal-to-keep-manufacturing-jobs-in-u-s
36. https://youtu.be/jvK2Q4dX4CQ?t=1m56s
37. https://www.vnews.com/Sunapee-Police-Will-Get-a-License-Plate-Reader-Other-N-H-Chiefs-Say-It-Isn-t-a-Priority-18117871
38. http://www.nhpr.org/post/license-plate-scanners-raise-privacy-concerns-do-they-help-police#stream/0
39. https://bradfordtaxinstitute.com/Free_Resources/Federal-Income-Tax-Rates.aspx
40. https://www.youtube.com/watch?v=koPmuEyP3a0
41. https://www.ncbi.nlm.nih.gov/pubmed/8477683
42. https://www.thesun.co.uk/news/2690395/unhinged-feminist-youtuber-issues-crazed-call-for-women-to-kill-all-male-babies-and-any-man-you-see-in-the-streets/
43. https://www.youtube.com/watch?time_continue=9&v=Nc24KfmwSao
44. https://archive.nytimes.com/www.nytimes.com/books/first/j/johnson-terror.html
45. https://www.engadget.com/2018/09/06/ibm-nypd-facial-recognition-surveillance-body-camera-footage/
46. https://citylimits.org/2016/10/18/city-eyes-massive-network-of-surveillance-cameras-yawn/
47. https://www.nydailynews.com/opinion/bryan-schonfeld-expand-nyc-surveillance-camera-network-article-1.2117122

48. https://arstechnica.com/tech-policy/2012/09/your-car-tracked-the-rapid-rise-of-license-plate-readers/
49. https://www1.nyc.gov/nyc-resources/service/2324/red-light-cameras
50. https://project.wnyc.org/speed-cameras/
51. https://nypost.com/2019/02/25/driver-dies-after-cops-take-him-for-dui-test-instead-of-hospital-lawyer/?fbclid=IwAR3nPPZ5XlUTIiR6j2iLS8qR8dTAtxJNADxi6jXIah-e6ctGFkp5GXx7hqo
52. https://www.youtube.com/watch?v=1clsPeXT9Io
53. http://thefreethoughtproject.com/police-union-cop-trying-shoot-autistic-man-not-caregiver-heroic/
54. https://www.latimes.com/nation/la-na-liang-sentencing-20160419-story.html
55. https://www.nationalreview.com/corner/police-murder-daniel-shaver/
56. https://www.youtube.com/watch?v=hDmMJViKo3g
57. https://thefreethoughtproject.com/cop-rapes-woman-jail-supervisors-video-threaten-kill-her-offer-taco/
58. https://thefreethoughtproject.com/school-cop-admits-raping-studnet-no-jail-doesnt-register-sex-offender/
59. https://www.thedailybeast.com/cop-accused-of-beating-three-wives-and-raping-a-blind-woman-didnt-lose-his-job-5
60. https://nypost.com/2018/02/20/teen-claims-she-was-handcuffed-while-cops-raped-her/
61. https://www.impactfund.org/social-justice-blog/structural-racism
62. https://www.chicagotribune.com/news/opinion/letters/chi-letters-police-are-just-doing-their-jobs-20141009-story.html
63. https://www.youtube.com/watch?v=Yc9bBTaU6NY
64. https://www.washingtontimes.com/news/2018/feb/23/deputy-scot-peterson-hid-while-students-were-shot-/
65. https://www.youtube.com/watch?v=JzY4FXYucbk
66. http://tribunist.com/news/supreme-court-ruling-police-have-no-duty-to-protect-the-general-public/
67. https://thefreethoughtproject.com/school-cop-arrested-for-blindfolding-and-brutally-raping-6-year-old-girl-in-a-classroom/
68. https://thefreethoughtproject.com/school-cop-teacher-rape-student/
69. https://www.net-abbey.org/hitler-as-god.htm
70. https://encyclopedia.ushmm.org/content/en/article/nazi-propaganda
71. https://dailyvoice.com/new-jersey/rutherford/police-fire/east-rutherford-supports-law-enforcement-with-blue-line-down-streets/682481/
72. https://www.rebelcircus.com/blog/school-cop-received-oral-sex-child-wont-register-sex-offender/
73. https://www.theroot.com/stop-and-frisk-across-america-1790896107
74. https://www.propublica.org/article/dna-dragnet-in-some-cities-police-go-from-stop-and-frisk-to-stop-and-spit
75. https://www.dailywire.com/news/26655/horrifying-ex-cop-testifies-baltimore-police-emily-zanotti
76. https://newyork.cbslocal.com/2016/04/18/nypd-scandal-arrest/
77. https://hotair.com/archives/2016/08/22/trump-clinton-foundation-most-corrupt-enterprise-in-political-history/
78. https://libertyblock.com/the-non-representative-republic/
79. https://thefederalistpapers.org/founders/jefferson/thomas-jefferson-danger-from-a-powerful-central-government
80. https://news.gallup.com/poll/197231/trump-clinton-finish-historically-poor-images.aspx
81. https://civiqs.com/results/track_country?annotations=true&net=false&uncertainty=true
82. https://www.youtube.com/watch?v=RCNd7h0fsdE&list=PLFFCA55326B642A4D&index=164&t=0s
83. https://www.nytimes.com/interactive/2019/us/abortion-laws-states.html
84. https://www.youtube.com/watch?v=bO9BBq92Eu4
85. https://www.buckeyefirearms.org/gun-quotations-founding-fathers
86. https://www.nydailynews.com/new-york/nyc-crime/cops-seek-sweatsuit-clad-man-shot-bystander-brooklyn-article-1.2242439
87. https://civiqs.com/results/gun_control?annotations=true&net=false&uncertainty=true
88. https://www.youtube.com/watch?v=rhBwHiLcTG8&t=1749s
89. https://libertyblock.com/what-is-a-grant/
90. https://eaglerising.com/61385/outrageous-ny-grade-school-hires-drag-queen-for-story-time-tells-kids-theres-no-such-thing-as-boy-and-girl/
91. https://granitegrok.com/blog/2019/05/school-teacher-tries-to-transgender-8-year-old-without-parents-knowledge-or-consent
92. https://www.intellectualtakeout.org/article/8th-place-high-school-girls-life-after-transgender-students-join-her-sport?fbclid=IwAR2OPmOzeX4SRovDJWHg9MyT8FcF9ynut-fv0VKSdy1e72RqgC4-oYeDm1k
93. https://www.congress.gov/bill/116th-congress/house-bill/5/text

94. https://civiqs.com/results/cannabis_legal
95. https://fee.org/articles/the-deadly-incompetence-of-the-fda
96. https://libertyblock.com/a-manchin-of-corruption/
97. https://fee.org/articles/feds-announce-they-will-stop-regulating-the-number-of-cherries-in-cherry-pies/?utm_source=zapier&fbclid=IwAR1Fkag5ATfW6Wx7D_cMxc0-d9dYv2beT3MNIKWOINuVUpb6x14Tlo2lfUk
98. https://www.hhs.gov/about/budget/fy2018/budget-in-brief/fda/index.html#ftno5
99. https://www.heritage.org/immigration/report/the-fiscal-cost-unlawful-immigrants-and-amnesty-the-us-taxpayer
100. https://civiqs.com/results/build_border_wall?annotations=true&net=false&uncertainty=true&home_state=California
101. https://civiqs.com/results/build_border_wall?annotations=true&net=false&uncertainty=true&home_state=Wyoming
102. https://civiqs.com/results/affordable_care_act?annotations=true&net=false&uncertainty=true
103. https://civiqs.com/results/gun_control?annotations=true&net=false&uncertainty=true
104. https://www.huffpost.com/entry/young-people-socialism_n_1175218
105. https://www.youtube.com/watch?v=ISsdSf0tjWM
106. https://www.nationalreview.com/2018/03/census-questions-illegal-immigrants-give-cities-political-power/
107. https://civiqs.com/results/favorable_democrats?annotations=true&net=false&uncertainty=true
108. http://www.cnn.com/interactive/2012/04/us/table.military.troops/
109. https://www.fool.com/taxes/2017/10/15/trump-tax-plan-what-the-death-of-the-estate-tax-re.aspx
110. https://www.cnn.com/2017/12/28/politics/andrew-cuomo-state-and-local-tax-deduction-cnntv/index.html
111. https://www.usatoday.com/story/news/nation-now/2018/01/03/cuomo-new-york-sue-over-federal-tax-law/1001655001/
112. http://libertyviral.com/the-top-5-reasons-why-fdr-sucked-as-president/#axzz56B2BTzPK
113. https://www.reclaimnewyork.org/2016/07/05/reclaimer-alert-governor-tries-bury-50-million-jobs-failure/
114. https://www.nytimes.com/2016/05/25/nyregion/a-tangle-of-interests-behind-cuomos-1-billion-boon-for-buffalo.html
115. https://libertyblock.com/the-law-abiding-citizen/
116. https://www.wired.com/2008/11/the-boy-who-cri/
117. https://libertyblock.com/do-traffic-laws-keep-make-us-safer/
118. https://libertyblock.com/nh-police-to-ditch-phones-mdts-motorcycles/
119. http://www.gencourt.state.nh.us/house/members/default.aspx
120. http://gencourt.state.nh.us/Senate/members/wml.aspx
121. https://new-hampshire.secure.force.com/support/GOV_Opinion
122. https://www.nh.gov/dot/contactus/index.htm
123. https://legiscan.com/NH/bill/HB1102/2020
124. https://www.fda.gov/food/food-additives-petitions/sodium-reduction
125. https://libertyblock.com/why-are-cigarettes-cheeseburgers-alcohol-still-legal/
126. https://legiscan.com/NH/bill/SB719/2020
127. https://www.criminaldefenselawyer.com/resources/new-hampshire-misdemeanor-crimes-class-and-sentences.
128. https://www.cdc.gov/vitalsigns/motor-vehicle-safety/index.html
129. https://lawcenter.giffords.org/resources/model-laws/